NOVEMBER
MONTHLY
ACTIVITIES

Written by Mary Ellen Sterling and Susan Schumann Nowlin

Illustrated by: Paula Spence, Keith Vasconcelles and Theresa Wright

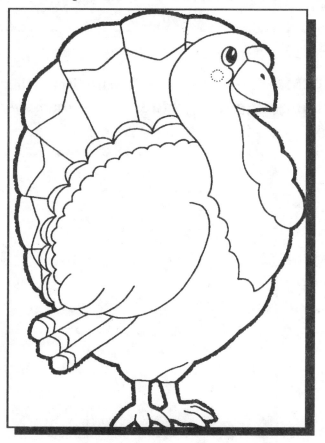

Teacher Created Materials, Inc.
P.O. Box 1040
Huntington Beach, CA 92647
©*1989 Teacher Created Materials, Inc.*
Made in U.S.A.

ISBN 1-55734-153-2

Table Of Contents

Table of Contents
(cont.)

Introduction

November Monthly Activities provides 80 dynamic pages of ready-to-use resources, ideas and activities that students love! All are centered around the themes, special dates and holidays of the month.

A complete "month-in-a-book," it includes:

- *A Calendar of Events* - ready to teach from and filled with fascinating information about monthly events, PLUS lots of fun ways you can apply these useful facts in your classroom.

- *A Whole Language Integrated Teaching Unit* - theme-based planning strategies, projects, lessons, activities, and more that provide a practical, yet imaginative approach to a favorite seasonal topic.

- *People, Places and Events* - an exciting series of activities that relate to the daily events in the Calendar of Events, and provide an innovative way for students to reinforce skills.

- *Management Pages* - a supply of reproducible pages that take you through the month, providing a wealth of valuable organizational aids that are right at your fingertips.

- *A Bulletin Board* - featuring a "hands-on" approach to learning; complete with full-size patterns, step-by-step directions, and tips for additional ways you can use the board.

Ideas and activities are also included for:

- *math*
- *art projects*
- *reading*
- *science*
- *geography*
- *social studies*
- *stationery*
- *creative writing*
- *literature ideas*
- *cooking*
- *reports*
- *seasonal words*

November Monthly Activities is the most complete seasonal book you'll ever find, and its convenient, reproducible pages will turn each month into a special teaching—and learning—experience!

Using The Pages

November Monthly Activities brings you a wealth of easy-to-use, fun-filled activities and ideas that will help you make the most of November's special themes and events. Although most of the activities are designed to be used within this month, if the holidays and traditions vary in your location, you may easily adapt the pages to fit your needs. Here are some tips for getting the most from your pages:

CALENDAR OF EVENTS

Each day makes note of a different holiday, tells about a famous person or presents a historical event. A question relating to each topic is provided (answers are on page 76). Teachers can use these facts in any number of ways including:

- *Post a copy of the calendar on a special bulletin board. Each day assign a different student to find the answer to that day's question. Set aside some time during the day to discuss the question with the whole class.*

- *Write the daily fact on the chalkboard. Have students keep a handwriting journal and copy the fact first thing each morning. They must use their best handwriting, of course!*

- *Use a daily event, holiday or famous person as a springboard for a Whole Language theme. Brainstorm with the class to find out what they already know about the topic. Explore the topic through literature, the arts, language and music.*

- *Older students can write a report on any of the daily topics. Younger students can be directed to draw a picture of the historical event or figure.*

- *Have students make up their own questions to go along with the day's event!*

- *Assign each student a different day of the calendar. Have them present a short oral report to the class on that day's topic.*

- *Use the daily events for math reinforcement. Ask how many: Days, weeks, months and years since the event occurred (for a real brain teaser, have students compute hours, minutes and seconds).*

- *Use in conjunction with the People, Places and Events section (pages 32 - 46).*

BLANK CALENDAR

Copy a calendar for each student. Have students use them to:

- *Write in daily assignments; check off each one as completed.*

- *Set daily goals—behavioral or academic.*

- *Copy homework assignments.*

- *Fill in with special dates, holidays, classroom or school events.*

- *Keep track of classroom chores.*

- *Use as a daily journal of feelings.*

- *Make ongoing lists of words to learn to spell.*

- *Answer the Question of the Day (see Calendar of Events).*

- *Record daily awards (stamps, stickers, etc.) for behavior or academic achievement.*

- *At the end of the day, evaluate their attitude, behavior, class work, etc. and give them a grade and explanation for the grade.*

- *Log reading time and number of pages read for free reading time.*

- *If there are learning centers in the classroom, let students keep track of work they have completed at each one or copy a schedule of times and days they may use the centers.*

- *Each day, write at least one new thing they learned.*

MANAGEMENT PAGES

Nifty ideas for extending the use of these pages.

- **Contracts** — *Help students set long or short term goals such as keeping a clean desk, reading extra books or improving behavior.*

- **Awards** — *Show students you appreciate them by giving awards for good attitude, helping, being considerate or for scholastic achievement. Students can give them to each other, their teacher or the principal!*

- **Invitations** — *Invite parents, grandparents, friends or another class to a classroom, school or sports event.*

- **Field Trip** — *Use for class trips or have students use in planning their own field trip to another country or planet.*

- **Supplies** — *Tell parents when you need art, craft, classroom, physical education or any other kind of supplies.*

- **Record Form** — *Place names in alphabetical order to keep track of classroom chores, completed assignments, contracts or permission slips.*

- **Stationery** — *Use as a creative writing pattern, for correspondence with parents, or for homework assignments.*

- **News** — *Fill in with upcoming weekly events and send home on Monday or let students fill in each day and take home on Friday. Younger students may draw a picture of something special they did or learned.*

- **Clip Art** — *Decorate worksheets, make your own stationery or answer pages. Enlarge and use for bulletin boards.*

Hot Tips!

 Be sure to look for the hot tips at the beginning of each section—they provide quick, easy and fun ways of extending the activities!

November Highlights

- Calendar of Events
- Spelling Activities
- Story Starters
- Gameboard
- Poetry
- Art Project
- And More!

Hot Tips!

 Since November 1 is National Author's Day, and two best-loved authors (Louisa May Alcott and Mark Twain) were born this month, celebrate with a special display of their books! Read selections from some of the books aloud to your class.

 Did you know the newspaper is an excellent source for patterns? Use an overhead projector to enlarge them.

NOVEMBER

November is the eleventh month of the year. Its name is derived from the Latin word novem which means nine. In the Roman calendar, November was the ninth month.

Flower: Chrysanthemum   Birthstone: Topaz

National Author's Day

1

Who is your favorite author?

Polish composer Paderewski was born in 1860.

6

What musical instrument did he play?

Marie Curie, a chemist and physicist was born in 1867.

7

What is a physicist?

In 1889 on this date Montana became the forty-first state.

8

What is the capital of Montana?

Elizabeth Cady Stanton was born in 1815.

12

Which amendment to the Constitution gave women the right to vote?

Birth date of Robert Louis Stevenson, 1850.

13

What is the meter of a poem?

French painter Claude Monet was born in 1840.

14

Did Monet prefer bright or dull colors in his paintings?

Abraham Lincoln delivered the Gettysburg Address in 1863.

19

How many years is fourscore?

Thanksgiving is a special day celebrated in November.

20

On which day of the week is Thanksgiving observed?

North Carolina became the twelfth state in 1789.

21

What is the state tree of North Carolina?

President John F. Kennedy was assassinated in Dallas, Texas in 1963.

22

What is the Peace Corps?

Civil rights leader Sojourner Truth, was born in 1790.

26

What is an abolitionist?

American historian Charles Beard was born in 1874.

27

What is the root word of historian?

The U.S.A. launched Mariner 4 in 1964 to take photos of Mars.

28

Why is Mars called the red planet?

Two states, North Dakota and South Dakota, were admitted to the union in 1889. **2** *Which of these two states has the larger population?*	Sandwich Day The sandwich was invented in 1762. **3** *What is your favorite sandwich?*	King Tut's tomb was discovered on this day in 1922. **4** *In what country was it found?*	Guy Fawkes Day (England) **5** *Who was Guy Fawkes?*
Benjamin Banneker, a black astronomer, was born on this day in 1731. **9** *What does an astronomer study?*		The Marine Corps was founded on this day in 1775. **10** *Why are Marines sometimes called leathernecks?*	Veterans Day (U.S.A.) Remembrance Day (Canada) **11** *What is a veteran?*
Shichi-Go-San (Japan) This festival is for boys who are 3 or 5 and for girls who are 3 or 7 years old. **15** *What is a kimono?*	Oklahoma became the 46th state in 1907. **16** *What is Oklahoma's state flower?*	Homemade Bread Day **17** *How many different kinds of bread can you name?*	Mickey Mouse's Birthday (Created in 1928.) **18** *How old is Mickey this year?*
Billy the Kid, a legendary outlaw, was born on this day in 1859. **23** *What is a legend?*		Junipero Serra, Spanish missionary, was born in 1713. **24** *Which California mission was the first one to be founded?*	Baseball star Joe DiMaggio was born in 1914. **25** *For which baseball team did he play?*
Author Louisa May Alcott was born in 1832. **29** *What is the name of her most famous novel?*	Birth date of author Mark Twain in 1835. **30** *What was Mark Twain's real name?*		Other holidays celebrated this month are: ■ *Election Day* ■ *Thanksgiving Day (4th Thursday in November)* ■ *Children's Book Week (3rd week in November)*

November

SUNDAY	MONDAY	TUESDAY	WEDNESDAY	THURSDAY	FRIDAY	SATURDAY

November Words and Activities

November Word Bank

election	Indians	Tuesday	pumpkin
town	gobble	Democrat	unknown
turkey	rights	Mayflower	state
candidates	governor	armistice	ballot
vote	maize	govern	blessings
country	veteran	Republican	honor
Pilgrims	November	colonists	city
Thanksgiving	president	tomb	officials
citizen	settlers	county	cornucopia
mayor	treaty	political	ceremonies

Spelling Activities

Give the students a choice of assignments below or have them try one of the following ideas in place of the standard spelling lesson.

- *Write the words in alternating colors of red, white, and blue. Or alternate the colors of the letters of each word using red, white, and blue.*

- *Draw a hat with a Vote band on it (or enlarge one of the hats from page 14). Write all the words that have to do with elections on the hat.*

- *Write only the words that have to do with Thanksgiving.*

- *Write ten sentences using two words from the November Word Bank in each sentence.*

- *Choose ten words. Change one letter in each word to make a new one. For example,*

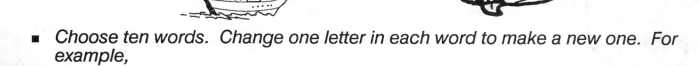

city → pity   **ballot → ballet**

Story Starters

☐ Thanksgiving is a special holiday celebrated in November by Americans. People take time to give thanks for all the good things they have. Encourage your students to give thanks, too. Group the students and instruct them to write some things they are thankful for. Then have them draw, color, or paint pictures to go with their words. Butcher paper can be used for a background or students can tear open a large grocery sack to use. Tear the edges for an antique look.

We Are Thankful...

| family friends | home food toys | school clothes |

 ☐ Since November is traditionally the month in which local, state, and national elections are held, you may want to encourage students to express their political views. Some research may be required before they begin writing.

- Our Voting Privilege
- Why I Am a Democrat/Republican/Other
- Why Twelve Year Olds Should/Should Not Be Allowed to Vote
- How to Get Elected (President, Mayor, etc.)

 ☐ Children's Book Week is celebrated in November. In honor of the occasion, have children do one or more of the following activities:

- Dress as their favorite book character.
- Write a short report about a children's author.
- Read or tell in their own words a favorite part of the story.
- Write a letter to their favorite author.
- Make a class chart of favorite books.

November Math

1. How many different triangles can you count?

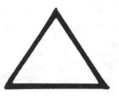

2. How many different squares can you count?

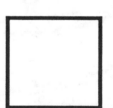

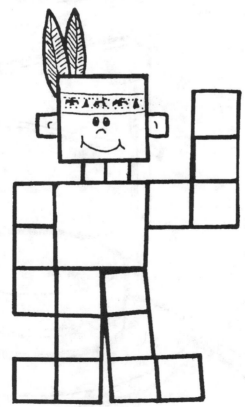

Name _____ **Skill** _____

November Worksheet

Directions: _____

1.

2.

3.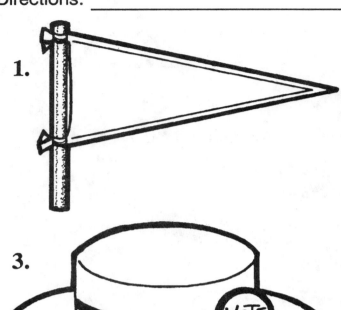

4.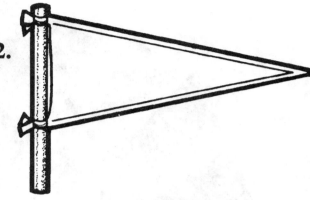

5.

6.

7.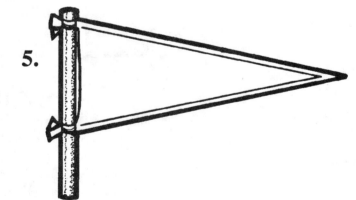

8.

Cornucopia Delight

Complete the names of the fruits and vegetables found in the cornucopia below.

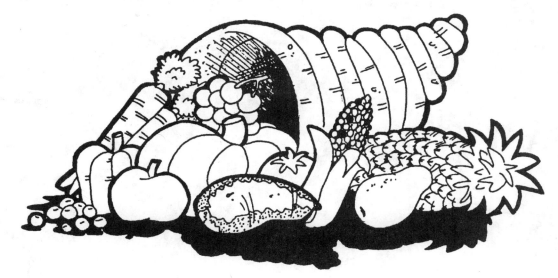

1. a __ __ __ e

2. p __ __ __ __ __ r

3. t __ __ __ __ o

4. c __ __ __ __ t

5. g __ __ e

6. p __ __ r

7. p __ __ __ __ __ n

8. c __ __ __ __ __ __ __ y

9. p __ __ __ __ o

10. p __ __ __ __ __ __ __ e

11. s __ __ __ __ h

12. c __ __ n

WORD BANK

pear	corn	pumpkin
tomato	squash	cranberry
pepper	apple	pineapple
grape	potato	carrot

Turkey Trot Gameboard

Use this generic gameboard for any subject area. Label each circle with a different math fact or science term or prefix, etc. (For more ideas see pages 79 and 80.) Each player will need a marker. Players can move one space at a time or can determine the number of spaces moved with a die.

Game Page

No-Clues Crossword Puzzle — An Indoor Game.

Draw a grid on the chalkboard or on the overhead projector. Determine a simple topic—sports, foods, holidays, etc. Explain to the students that they will be making a crossword puzzle without clues. Divide the group into two teams. The first person from Team 1 writes a word related to the chosen category onto the grid. If the word is spelled correctly, he gets three points for his team. If the word is spelled incorrectly, a teammate may try to correct it and get one point for his team. Set a maximum of three tries to spell a word correctly after which no points are given.

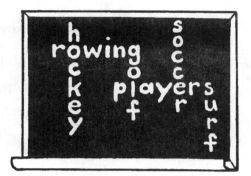

Then, the first player on the second team writes a related word and attaches it to the word on the grid. Play continues to go back and forth between teams as they attach words in a crossword puzzle configuration. The first team to get twenty-one or more points wins.

On Your Mark — An Outdoor Game

For this variation of follow-the-leader, cut out squares of cardboard to use as markers; make one for each child, minus one (the leader in this game does not get a marker). Have the students stand in a circle; one foot should be on the marker. Choose an extra player to be the leader. As the leader moves around the circle, he taps different players on the shoulder and tells them to follow him. Once all players have been chosen, they must hop, skip, do jumping jacks, run in place, etc. just as the leader does. When the guide gives a signal (he can yell, "Places," or "Run Home!") the players are to run back to the circle and find a marker. The child left without a marker chooses someone else to be the new leader. Or, make the first one back to a place in the circle the new leader; the child without a marker would take his place in the circle.

Poetry Page

- **Diamond Poems.** Write a poem in a diamond shape using the following format:

Bread
Fresh, soft
Rising, baking, cooling
I love the smell.
Loaf

noun

adjective, adjective

verb, verb, verb

a short line about the poem

synonym for first line

- **Noun Poems.** This is a good way to review or reinforce nouns. After discussing the definition of NOUN and brainstorming lists of nouns, have students group them into categories. For example, the category Animals might contain the words lion, giraffe, squirrel, penguin, dog, etc. Have the students choose a category and write a noun poem with words from that category. For example,

Squirrel

Bird

Rabbit

Forest

Elephants

Clowns

Popcorn

Circus

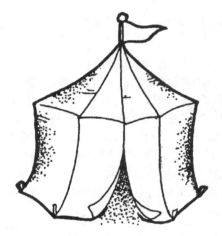

- **Grab Bag Poems.** Place one small item in a lunch sack. Prepare one for each student and fill with items such as cooking utensils (spatula, wood spoon, measuring cups, etc.); cleaning items (sponge, empty spray bottle, bar of soap, etc.); personal hygiene items (toothbrush, comb, washcloth, etc.); small toys (marbles, cars, rubber ball, etc.). Let each child choose a sack. He must write a poem about the object in his bag. Note: It might be helpful to have children list two or three words that rhyme with their object before they begin to write. Grab bags may contain pictures rather than actual objects.

18

A-Maizing Art

Materials:

Scissors; tagboard; glue; colored popcorn or 1/4'' squares of yellow, orange, and brown construction paper; maize shape; brown crepe paper or construction paper.

Directions:

Cut out the maize shape and glue to tagboard. Glue colored popcorn or construction paper squares to the shape. Make two or three husks from brown construction paper. Attach these husks to the back of the maize.

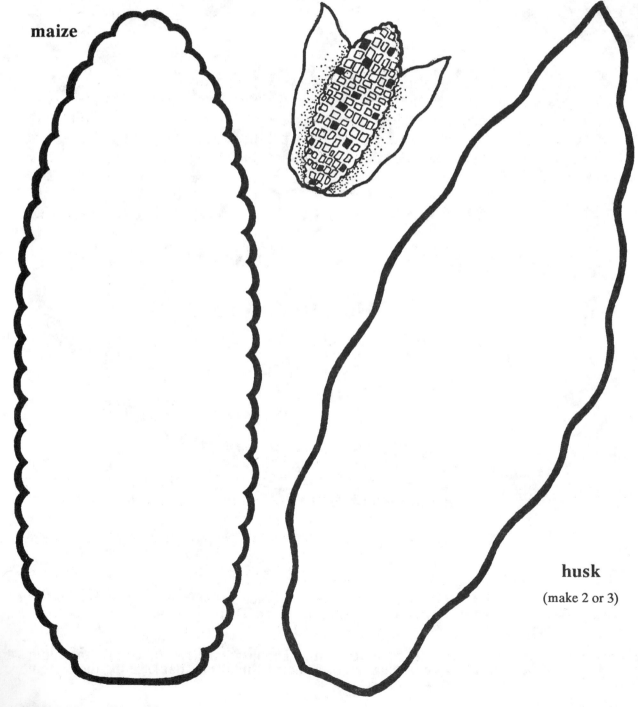

maize

husk

(make 2 or 3)

November
Whole
Language Unit:
THANKSGIVING CORNUCOPIA

- ○ **How to Write a Unit**
- ○ **Lessons**
- ○ **Worksheets**
- ○ **And More!**

Hot Tips!

 For homework, assign students to bring in interesting pictures of fruits, vegetables, and other fall foods. Reward each student who brings a picture with a Thanksgiving clip art cut-out, or with an award (see page 56).

Read a book to the class that tells about the first Thanksgiving and the conditions under which the Pilgrims lived. Make a Venn diagram or a chart comparing Thanksgiving then and now.

How to Plan

In the U.S.A. the fourth Thursday of November is set aside as a day of Thanksgiving in commemoration of the Pilgrims who first held a special feast in 1621. It wasn't until President Lincoln's term that Thanksgiving was proclaimed a national holiday. Today, it is an important annual event. A study unit based on Thanksgiving would provide ample opportunities for learning. Begin your unit by following these step-by-step guidelines.

 1. Set the mood in your classroom with an appropriate bulletin board. Pages 69 to 75 contain all the patterns you'll need to create a Thanksgiving display (see diagram below). Fruits should be left blank for now; they can be labeled after brainstorming with the students.

 2. Assemble your resources: Books, films, tapes, games, texts, and real objects.

 3. Plan general lessons integrating math, reading, art, music, language, and science.

 4. Outline your lesson goals and objectives.

 5. Make evaluation tools that are appropriate for the lesson.

 6. After the first week of lessons, evaluate and then plan the next week.

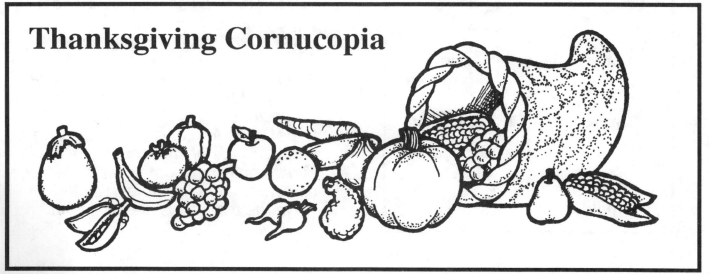

Thanksgiving Cornucopia

Projects and Lessons

The following pages describe specific lessons and ideas that can be used to integrate the curriculum through the study of Thanksgiving.

- **Set up a display table** *with a cornucopia and various fruits and vegetables, especially those used in the first Thanksgiving feast (chestnuts, corn, popcorn, cranberries, pumpkin, squash, etc.). Also include some books on Thanksgiving. Read related stories and poems aloud to the class.*

- **Keep parents informed** *about the class' upcoming activities. Compose a class letter to send home and have students copy the message on their own stationery (see diagram at right). Use the letter to enlist volunteers or request any necessary supplies you'll be needing throughout this unit.*

Language

- **Brainstorm with the students.** *Find out what they already know about Thanksgiving. List all the appropriate responses on the chalkboard or a flip chart. Use these ideas to plan specific lessons. Hint: You may want to record vocabulary words on the fruits of the Thanksgiving Cornucopia bulletin board.*

Fruits	Vegetables
tomato	corn
apple	squash

Science

- **Display a cornucopia.** *Have students bring in actual samples of fresh fruits and vegetables to fill the horn of plenty. (Pictures can be used instead of fresh samples). Make a class chart with two headings: Fruits and Vegetables (see diagram at left). Group the contents of the cornucopia into the two headings. Students can draw pictures or cut pictures from magazines to put onto the chart. Label each fruit and vegetable. Have small groups of students make a similar chart, this time comparing one fruit with one vegetable. List all the ways the two foods are different.*

Projects and Lessons

Social Studies and Science

- **Group students** *to research those foods that were newly introduced to the Pilgrim settlers by the Indians (popcorn, squash, peppers, peanuts, potatoes, tomatoes, corn, etc.). Find out how and where they grow; find out different ways to prepare these foods. (For help in writing a report see page 30.) Bring in samples of fresh vegetables to make soup. Fix an easy breakfast favorite of the early settlers—popcorn and cream. Make a modern version of succotash (recipe is on page 25).*

Art

- **Cornucopia Mobile.** *Use the cornucopia and fruit patterns from the Bulletin Board on pages 69 to 75. Duplicate patterns onto tagboard. Color and cut out. Or, glue fabric scraps to each pattern piece. Or, spread white glue on each pattern; sprinkle with unsweetened soft drink powder and rub it in. After drying, it can be rubbed and smelled! Connect and hang the pieces with yarn or string (see diagram at left).*

Language

- **Give each student a different shape** *(use patterns from the Cornucopia Bulletin Board pages 69 to 75). Have them list three things for which they are thankful. Fill your cornucopia bulletin board with all the I Am Thankful lists.*

Language and Math

- **Make a class graph** *of Thanksgiving favorites. Brainstorm a list of traditional Thanksgiving dishes. Vote on class favorites. Have small groups make another graph, this time polling another class on their favorite foods. Compare all the graphs. Which food is the best-liked? Least-liked? Which class liked corn the most? Which class voted the same amount for two different foods? How many people voted for corn altogether?*

Mrs. Green					Rm. 11
Thanksgiving Favorites					
corn	green beans	stuffing	pumpkin	sweet potatoes	cran-berries

Mr. Thompson					Rm. 8
Thanksgiving Favorites					
corn	green beans	stuffing	pumpkin	sweet potatoes	cran-berries

Projects and Lessons

Language

- **Read the poem** *Thanksgiving Day by Lydia Maria Child to the class. Discuss with students the various means of transportation they use to get to their grandparents' home. Have the students write and illustrate their own poem or story about going to their grandparents.*

Social Studies & Art

- **Cornucopia Award.** *Reduce the cornucopia pattern (pages 71 and 72) so that it fits on an 8 1/2 x 11 inch sheet of paper. Duplicate and give one to each student. Each day throughout November, have students make a different fruit or vegetable for his cornucopia. On each food shape, the student should write one thing for which he is proud of himself or tell one good thing he did for someone else. By the end of the month, each student will be more than proud to show off his horn of plenty!*

Science and Math

- **Gather a variety of fall vegetables,** *all about the same size. Group the students (make sure that the mix includes some stronger with some weaker academic abilities). Have each group estimate the weight of each vegetable and then actually weigh them. Estimates and actual weights should be recorded on a chart (see diagram below). Draw pictures or cut out pictures from magazines. Use graph on page 50.*

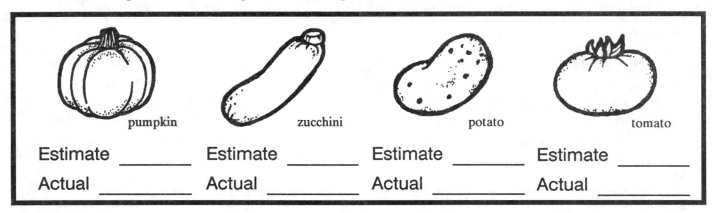

| pumpkin | zucchini | potato | tomato |

Estimate _____   Estimate _____   Estimate _____   Estimate _____

Actual _____   Actual _____   Actual _____   Actual _____

Language

- **Have students work in pairs.** *Give each pair a cornucopia shape (see page 31) or have them draw a cornucopia on an 8 1/2 x 11 inch sheet of paper. Inside the cornucopia they are to list as many things as they can think of that are small enough to fit inside their cornucopia. Some examples are a toothbrush, a mouse, six jellybeans, an orange, etc.*

Succotash

Some of the words in the recipe below are scrambled. Unscramble the underlined words and write them correctly on the lines.

When succotash was served at the *stirf* [1] __ i __ __ __

Thanksgiving dinner, it probably included *serfh* [2] __ r __ __ __

corn cut from the *ocb* [3] __ __ __ , bear grease,

tema [4] m __ __ __ , and kidney *snabe* [5] __ __ __ n __ .

Prepare a modern version using the following ingredients. You will also

need a pan, a *nopos* [6] __ __ o __ __ , and a hot

talep [7] __ l __ __ __ .

Cook one package of frozen *mila* [8] __ i __ __ beans and one

package of frozen cut *nocr* [9] __ __ r __ according to package

directions. Drain. Add 1/2 cup *mecra* [10] __ __ __ __ m ,

1/2 stick of *rutteb* [11] __ __ __ __ e __ , and salt and

eppepr [12] __ e __ __ __ __ to taste. Stir until heated through.

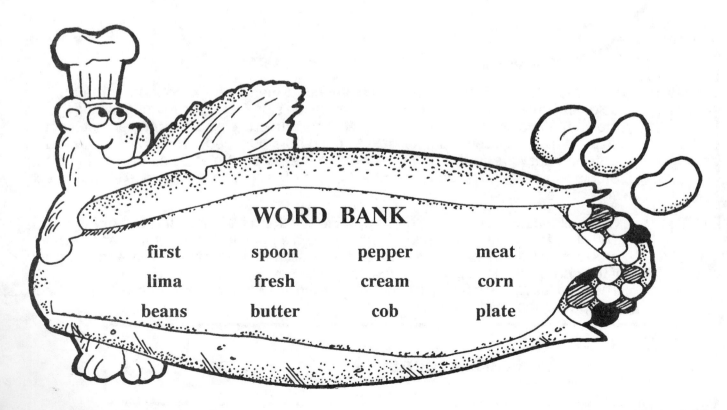

WORD BANK

first	spoon	pepper	meat
lima	fresh	cream	corn
beans	butter	cob	plate

Math Facts Review

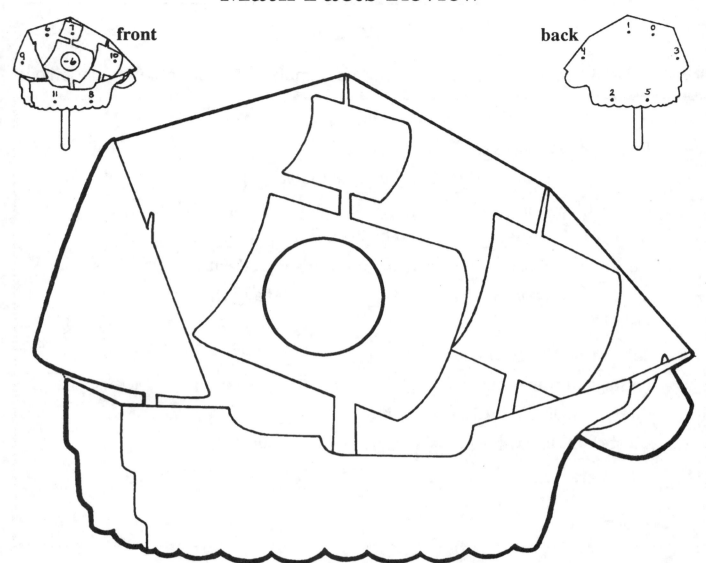

front

back

Directions: Make as many ship shapes as you will need. Glue to heavy tagboard for durability; color and cut out. In the circle write an operation sign (see operation signs below) and the number you want to review (see diagram). Punch holes along the perimeter of the ship. Write a different number next to each hole punched. Turn the ship over and write the answers to the problems next to the proper hole. Laminate and cut out. Staple two craft sticks together to the bottom of each ship placing one stick on each side of the ship.

To Play: One child faces the front of the ship, while another child faces the back of the ship. The child facing the front puts a pencil through a hole next to a number and says the problem aloud. (In the diagram, for example, six will be subtracted from each number. If the child puts the pencil in the ten, he would say, "Ten take away six equals four.") The child facing the back of the ship checks the answers. After all problems have been computed, the children trade places.

Operation Signs: $+$, $-$, $\times$, $\div$

Name _____   Date _____

Peppers Galore

Use the chart below to answer the questions.

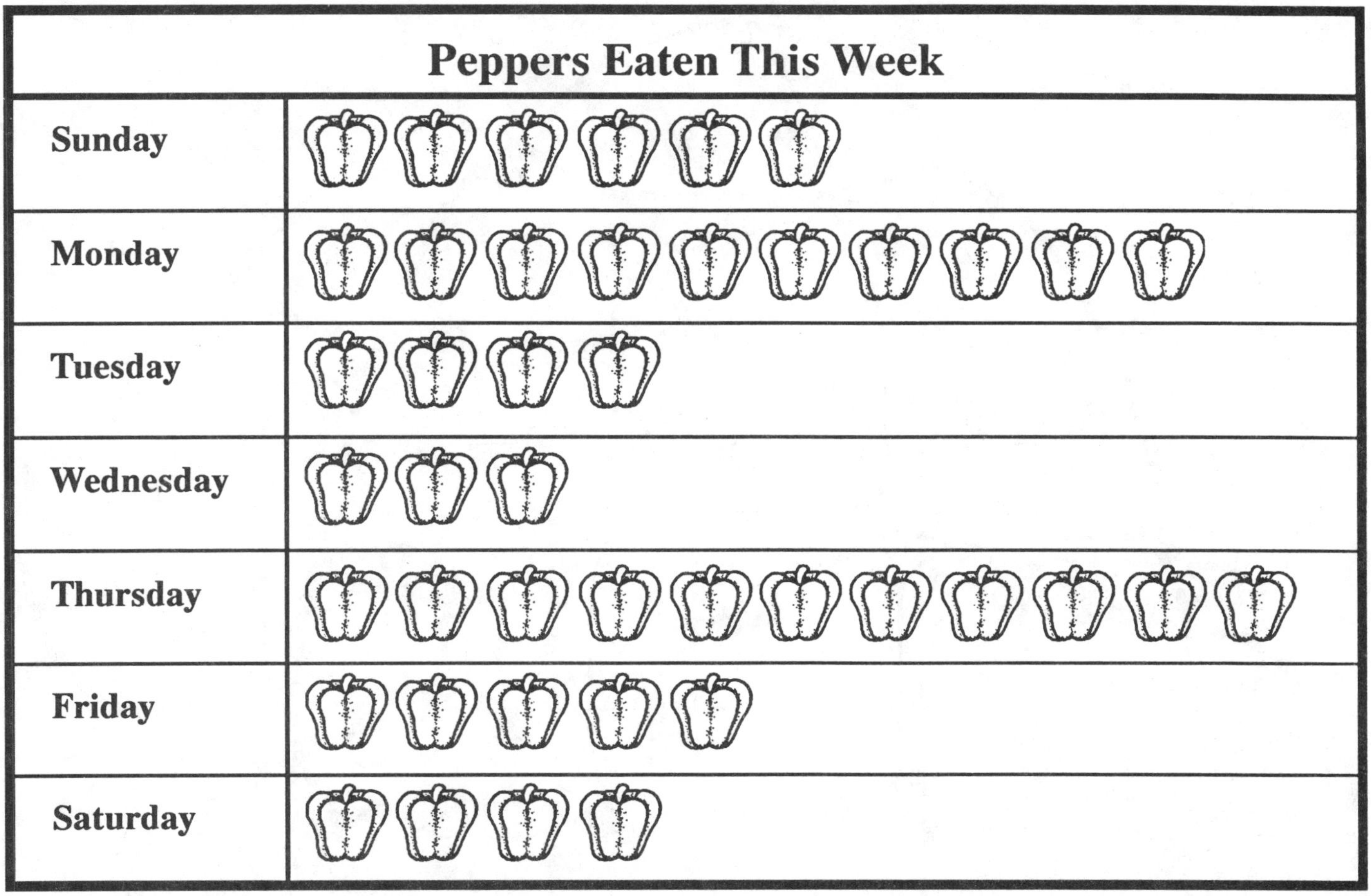

Peppers Eaten This Week	
Sunday	🫑🫑🫑🫑🫑🫑
Monday	🫑🫑🫑🫑🫑🫑🫑🫑🫑🫑
Tuesday	🫑🫑🫑🫑
Wednesday	🫑🫑🫑
Thursday	🫑🫑🫑🫑🫑🫑🫑🫑🫑🫑🫑🫑
Friday	🫑🫑🫑🫑🫑
Saturday	🫑🫑🫑🫑

1. How many peppers were eaten on Monday? _____

2. How many peppers were eaten on Wednesday? _____

3. On which day were the most peppers eaten? _____

4. On which day were the least number of peppers eaten? _____

5. On which two days were the same number of peppers eaten? _____

6. How many more peppers were eaten on Thursday than on Sunday? _____

7. How many peppers were eaten altogether on Monday and Friday? _____

8. How many peppers were eaten Sunday through Tuesday? _____

Challenge: How many peppers were eaten the whole week?

Date _____

Math Maize

Fill in the blanks with < or >. Color > purple. Color < yellow.

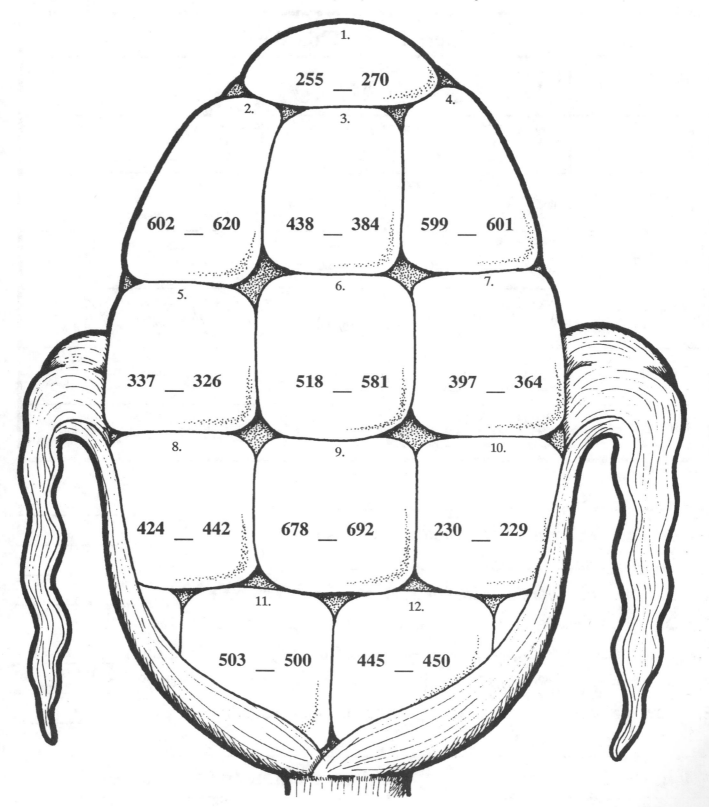

1.

255 __ 270

2.

602 __ 620

3.

438 __ 384

4.

599 __ 601

5.

337 __ 326

6.

518 __ 581

7.

397 __ 364

8.

424 __ 442

9.

678 __ 692

10.

230 __ 229

11.

503 __ 500

12.

445 __ 450

Name _____ **Skill** _____

Open Worksheet

Directions: _____

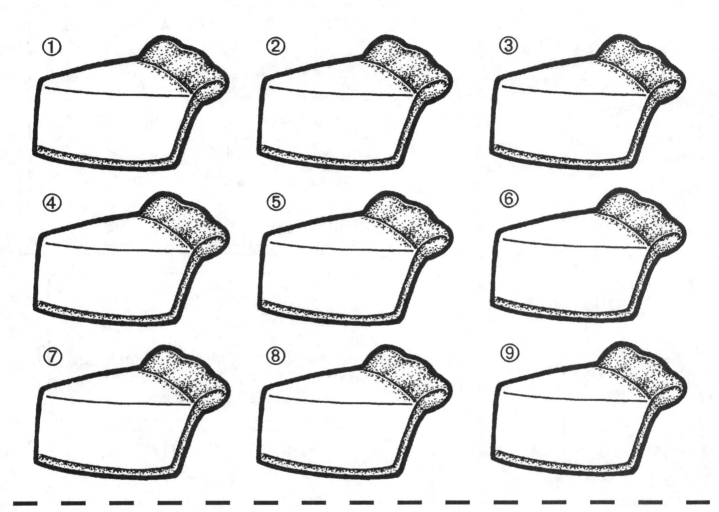

Answers

Name _____ Date _____

How to Write a Report

Use the steps outlined in this linear spiral to help you write a report.

CHOOSE A TOPIC

Keep it specific. VEGETABLES is too general; PUMPKIN is a specific vegetable.

WRITE FIVE QUESTIONS ABOUT THE TOPIC

1. What is your favorite pumpkin recipe?
2. What are some varieties of pumpkin?
3. How do pumpkins grow?
4. What are some ways to prepare pumpkins?
5. What are pumpkins?

PUT THE QUESTIONS IN GOOD ORDER

5.
2.
3.
4.
1.

DO RESEARCH

Use a variety of books: Texts, biographies, encyclopedias, and other reference books. Write notes on index cards.

WRITE THE REPORT

Write four or five sentences about each of the five questions.

BIBLIOGRAPHY

At the end of your report write the title and author of all the books you researched.

YOUR TURN

- Choose a topic and write it on the line. _____

- Write five questions about the topic.

  1. _____
  2 _____
  3. _____
  4. _____
  5. _____

- Put the questions in good order.

  1st _____ 2nd _____ 3rd _____ 4th _____ 5th _____

- Now you are ready to do your research, write a report and bibliography.

Creative Writing Pattern

Use this shape to record words that the class or small groups of students compile in brainstorming sessions. The cornucopia can also be used for cooperative stories or individual writing.

November
People, Places, and Events

- ○ **Election Day**
- ○ **Veterans Day**
- ○ **Thanksgiving**
- ○ **Children's Book Week**
- ○ **And More!**

The learning pages and ideas in this section are extensions of the people, places, and events from this month's calendar. They can be used to introduce a topic, reinforce, or follow-up a lesson, or as independent projects. Many of these activities can easily be incorporated into your Whole Language program; others are suitable for cooperative learning projects.

Hot Tips!

 November 21 is World Hello Day. Teach your students how to say "hello" in a different language. If you have bilingual students have them teach the class how to say "hello" in their language.

People in the United States and Canada celebrate Thanksgiving Day. In England, it is Harvest Home Day. In Japan, it is Labor Thanksgiving Day. Have the students research the Thanksgiving customs of England and Japan. How are they similar to the U.S. and Canada? How are they different?

We Remember

(Veterans Day - November 11)

> In the United States it is called Veterans Day. In Canada it is called Remembrance Day. In France and Great Britain, it is called Armistice Day. No matter what name you use, November 11 is the anniversary of the signing of the treaty in 1918 to end World War I. On this day many nations honor those who died for their country.
>
> The United States holds special ceremonies at Arlington National Cemetery in Virginia. There, at the Tomb of the Unknowns, two minutes of silence are observed followed by the bugle playing of taps. Then, a wreath is placed at the tomb, the burial place of four unknown Americans from World War I, World War II, the Korean War, and the Vietnam War.

1. **Knowledge**
   How did Armistice Day come to be known as Veterans Day in the United States? What is Veterans day called in Canada?

2. **Comprehension**
   In your own words, describe the special ceremonies held at Arlington National Cemetery every Veterans Day.

3. **Application**
   Illustrate any of the activities that take place during the Veterans Day ceremonies at Arlington National Cemetery.

4. **Analysis**
   Memorial Day also honors soldiers. Research this holiday to find out how it differs from Veterans Day.

5. **Synthesis**
   Write a poem about Veterans Day.

6. **Evaluation**
   Write a paragraph explaining the importance of Veterans Day and what it means to Americans.

Children's Books

(Children's Book Week)

Build a shelf of book words. Add a word from the Word Bank to make words that fit the clues.

WORD BANK

shelf

keeper

let

end

store

binder

mark

case

worm

mobile

1. book _____   A place to buy books.

2. book _____   This helps keep books upright.

3. book _____   One who puts the pages of a book together.

4. book _____   A small book.

5. book _____   Someone who reads a lot of books.

6. book _____   A set of shelves to hold books.

7. book _____   This is placed between book pages.

8. book _____   One who keeps business records.

9. book _____   A library that travels in a truck.

10. book _____   This holds books.

Challenge: Write all ten book words that you made above in alphabetical order!

Name _____   **Date** _____

Five States

Five states were admitted to the United States in the month of November but during different years. Label each outline below with its name and capital city. Some clues are given to help you.

1. This state is home to Mt. Rushmore.

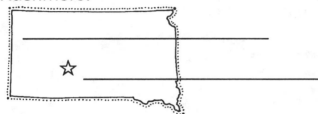

2. This is the home of Glacier National Park.

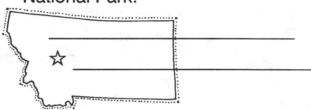

3. The National Cowboy Hall of Fame is in its capital.

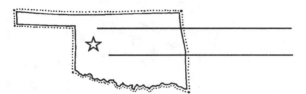

4. The Wright brothers flew the first airplane at Kitty Hawk.

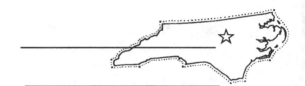

5. At Amidon you can see the burning coal beds.

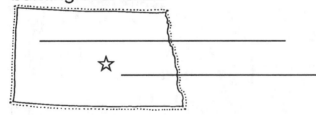

Write the number of the state next to each fact below.

a. Part of Yellowstone National Park is in this state. _____

b. The Badlands have many strange stone shapes; fossils are buried there. _____

c. Indian picture writing decorates Writing Rock. _____

d. This state is named for King Charles I of England. _____

e. Its state nickname is the "Sooner State." _____

Name _____ Date _____

The Sandwich

(Earl of Sandwich, November 3)

In 1762 John Montague, the fourth Earl of Sandwich, told his servant to prepare him a meal by placing a piece of meat between two slices of bread. The sandwich was born, and ever since then it has remained one of the most popular foods in the world.

Finish making the following sandwiches by writing in the correct letters.

1. ham and S __ __ __ __

2. bacon, lettuce, and t __ __ __ __ __

3. peanut butter and j __ __ __ __

4. corned beef on r __ __

5. fried e __ __

6. grilled c __ __ __ __ __

7. chicken fried s __ __ __ __

8. patty m __ __ __

9. c __ __ __

10. roast b __ __ __

11. filet of f __ __ __

12. tuna s __ __ __ __

WORD BANK

rye
steak
tomato
club

melt
beef
jelly
salad

Swiss
cheese
egg
fish

Name _____ **Date** _____

A Musical Lesson

(Paderewski, November 6)

Ignace Jan Paderewski was a Polish musician and composer. He lived from 1860 to 1941 and wrote music for violin and piano.

See how well you can read the music paragraph below. The clue at the beginning of each sentence will help you. (For more help, see the symbols in the keyboard at the bottom of the page.)

1. Music is written on a music __ __ __ __ __ which has five lines and four spaces.

2. A treble __ __ __ __ is a sign written at the beginning of the staff.

3. Music is divided into __ __ __ __ __ __ __s on the staff by bar lines.

4. A __ __ __ __ __ __ __ bar line is used to show when the music is done.

5. A __ __ __ __ __ note gets four beats per note.

6. A __ __ __ __ __ note gets two beats per note.

7. A __ __ __ __ __ __ __ note gets one beat per note.

8. A quarter __ __ __ __ is silent, but still gets counted as one beat.

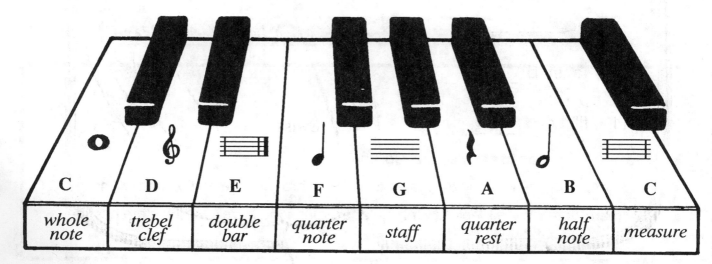

Election Day

Read the paragraph below to learn about Election Day. Then find the underlined words in the wordsearch puzzle. Words may be across, down, backwards, or diagonal.

<u>Election</u> Day is generally held on the first <u>Tuesday</u> after the first <u>Monday</u> in <u>November</u>. On this day, all U.S. <u>citizens</u> 18 years of age or older have the <u>right</u> to <u>vote</u>. However, they must meet certain <u>requirements</u> before they can actually cast a <u>ballot</u>. <u>Local</u>, <u>state</u>, and <u>federal</u> <u>officials</u> are voted upon as well as some local laws.

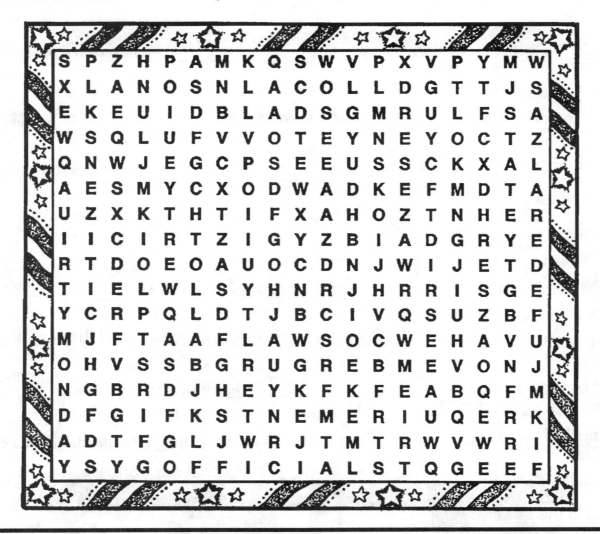

Research Topics

- What is the Electoral College?

- What is the function of the Electoral College?

- What determines how many delegates to the Electoral College that a state will have?

- How many votes in the Electoral College does your state have? Which state has the most? Which state has the least?

Astronomy Crossword Puzzle

(Benjamin Banneker, November 9)

An astronomer is a scientist who studies the planets, moons, and stars of our universe. Use the names of the members of our solar system in the Word Bank to fill in the crossword puzzle.

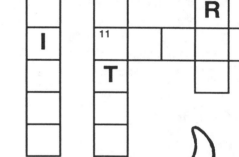

ACROSS

2. This planet is closest to the sun.

3. This planet rotates vertically instead of horizontally.

5. It is called the red planet because of its rust colored dust.

8. Beautiful rings surround this planet.

10. Halley's is a famous one.

11. This is the smallest planet.

DOWN

1. It is sometimes called the Morning Star or Evening Star.

4. The sun is one.

5. It orbits the earth.

6. This is the largest planet.

7. This planet supports life.

9. It is the eighth planet in our solar system.

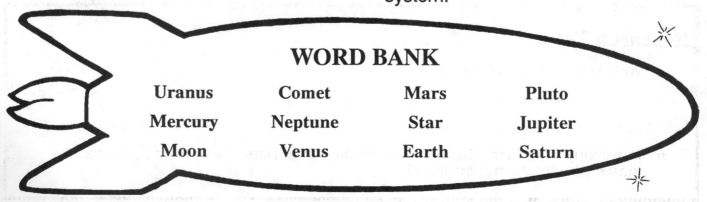

WORD BANK

Uranus	Comet	Mars	Pluto
Mercury	Neptune	Star	Jupiter
Moon	Venus	Earth	Saturn

November Greats

All of the people listed below are honored during the month of November. Find out their occupations by doing the math under the blanks and using the answers as a code to fill in the letters.

e = 16	m = 26	n = 10	o = 34	p = 24
u = 28	s = 14	d = 18	y = 22	t = 30
c = 8	h = 36	a = 12	i = 32	r = 20

1. Marie Curie

    ____ ____ ____ ____ ____ ____ ____
    24 ÷ 3 18 × 2 48 ÷ 3 13 × 2 15 + 17 28 ÷ 2 6 × 5

2. Claude Monet

    ____ ____ ____ ____ ____ ____ ____
    48 ÷ 2 60 ÷ 5 16 × 2 100 ÷ 10 15 × 2 32 ÷ 2 10 × 2

3. Junipero Serra

    ____ ____ ____ ____ ____ ____ ____ ____ ____ ____
    2 × 13 18 + 14 28 ÷ 2 2 × 7 64 ÷ 2 18 + 16 50 ÷ 5 48 ÷ 4 10 × 2 44 ÷ 2

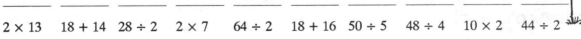

4. Louisa May Alcott

    ____ ____ ____ ____ ____ ____
    72 ÷ 6 4 × 7 60 ÷ 2 9 × 4 2 × 17 60 ÷ 3

5. Paderewski

    ____ ____ ____ ____ ____ ____ ____ ____
    48 ÷ 6 19 + 15 12 + 14 2 × 12 17 × 2 52 ÷ 3 32 ÷ 2 100 ÷ 5

Name _____   **Date** _____

Flag Math

(Veterans Day, November 11)

First tell which operation (addition, subtraction, multiplication, or division) you must use to work the problem. Then solve it; be sure to show all your work.

1. The first U.S. flag had 13 stars. Today's flag has 50. How many more stars does the U.S. flag have now?

    operation _____

    answer _____

2. Our flag has seven red stripes and six white stripes. How many stripes does the flag have altogether?

    operation _____

    answer _____

3. On June 14, 1777 the Stars and Stripes was adopted as the official U.S. flag. How many years ago was that?

    operation _____

    answer _____

4. There are fifty stars on one U.S. flag. How many stars are there on 12 flags?

    operation _____

    answer _____

5. The flag has five rows of stars and there are 50 stars altogether. How many stars are in each row?

    operation _____

    answer _____

6. If there were 60 stars on the flag and there were four rows, how many stars would there be in each row?

    operation _____

    answer _____

Kimono Art

(Shichi-Go-San, November 15)

In Japan, boys who are three or five years old and girls who are three or seven take part in an ancient festival called Shichi-Go-San. The children wear their traditional kimonos and go with their families to a shrine to worship.

Decorate your own kimono below with Japanese letters, flowers or symbols. Add a piece of fabric or colored construction paper for a sash.

Thanksgiving Day

(Last Thursday in November)

Read the poem below. Then circle the correct homonym in each parenthesis.

1. Over the river and (threw, through) the wood,
2. To Grandfather's house (we, wee) go,
3. The (horse, hoarse) knows the (weigh, way)
4. (Two, To) carry the (slay, sleigh)
5. (Through, Threw) the white and drifted snow.
6. Over the river and through the (would, wood),
7. Oh, how the wind does blow!
8. It stings the (toes, tows)
9. And bites the (knows, nose)
10. As over the ground we go.

Use words from the poem above to find rhymes for the words below.

pay

1. _____
2. _____

flow

1. _____
2. _____
3. _____

hose

1. _____
2. _____
3. _____

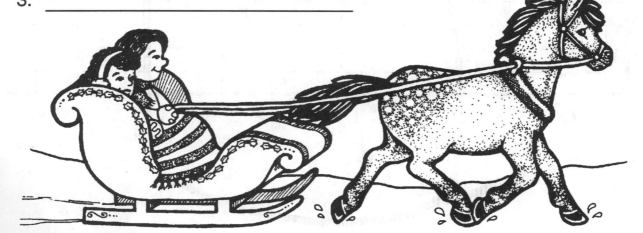

Date _____

Thanksgiving Graphics

(Thanksgiving Day)

Do the problems on the opposite page. Then coordinate the letter and the number on the grid below and write an "x" in the box. Some have been done for you. When you are finished, you will have a Thanksgiving picture. Color your picture.

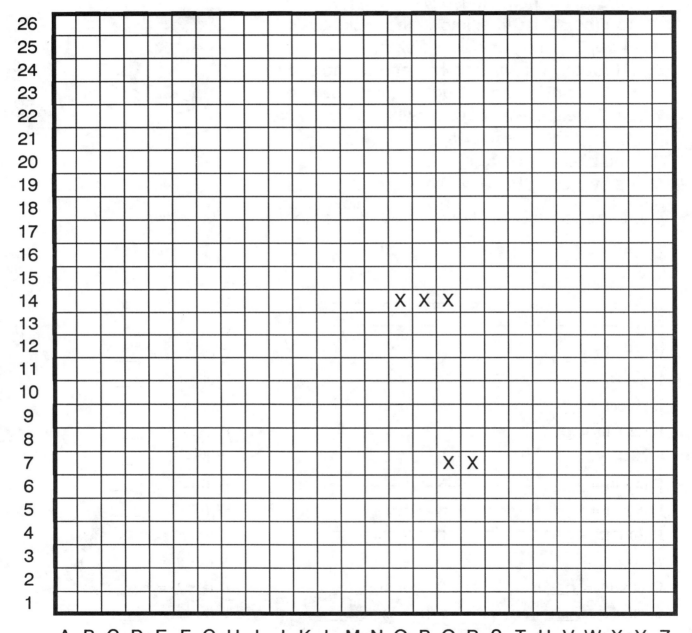

Thanksgiving Graphics

(cont.)

Solve each problem below. Coordinate the letter with the number answer. Find the
square and write an "x" in the box.

C (10 × 2) = _____   **I** (0 + 5) = _____   **Q** (15 + 6) = _____

C (8 + 11) = _____   **I** (28 ÷ 2) = _____   **Q** (4 + 9) = _____

D (4 × 5) = _____   **I** (2 × 9) = _____   **Q** (6 × 2) = _____

D (25 − 6) = _____   **I** (12 + 7) = _____   **Q** (8 + 3) = _____

E (30 ÷ 6) = _____   **I** (16 + 4) = _____   **Q** (40 ÷ 4) = _____

E (12 ÷ 2) = _____   **I** (7 × 3) = _____   **Q** (45 ÷ 5) = _____

E (15 − 8) = _____   **I** (5 + 17) = _____   **Q** (24 ÷ 3) = _____

E (4 × 2) = _____   **J** (12 ÷ 4) = _____   **R** (14 + 9) = _____

E (3 × 3) = _____   **J** (16 − 11) = _____   **S** (11 + 12) = _____

E (50 ÷ 5) = _____   **J** (7 × 2) = _____   **S** (21 ÷ 3) = _____

E (22 ÷ 2) = _____   **K** (6 + 8) = _____   **T** (30 − 7) = _____

E (3 × 4) = _____   **K** (2 × 2) = _____   **T** (14 ÷ 2) = _____

E (5 + 8) = _____   **K** (27 ÷ 9) = _____   **U** (13 + 10) = _____

E (2 × 7) = _____   **L** (35 ÷ 7) = _____   **U** (6 + 1) = _____

E (6 × 3) = _____   **L** (12 + 2) = _____   **V** (18 + 3) = _____

E (3 × 7) = _____   **M** (5 + 9) = _____   **V** (5 + 17) = _____

E (11 + 11) = _____   **M** (10 ÷ 2) = _____   **V** (18 − 11) = _____

F (12 + 10) = _____   **N** (40 ÷ 8) = _____   **W** (12 − 4) = _____

F (34 ÷ 2) = _____   **N** (21 − 7) = _____   **W** (3 + 6) = _____

F (2 × 8) = _____   **N** (9 + 6) = _____   **W** (26 − 7) = _____

F (5 × 3) = _____   **N** (32 ÷ 2) = _____   **W** (15 + 5) = _____

F (60 ÷ 12) = _____   **O** (4 + 1) = _____   **X** (6 + 12) = _____

G (11 × 2) = _____   **O** (9 + 8) = _____   **X** (2 + 9) = _____

G (2 × 10) = _____   **O** (36 ÷ 2) = _____   **X** (5 × 2) = _____

G (25 ÷ 5) = _____   **P** (14 − 9) = _____   **Y** (24 ÷ 2) = _____

H (18 + 4) = _____   **P** (27 − 8) = _____   **Y** (7 + 6) = _____

H (9 + 8) = _____   **P** (60 ÷ 3) = _____   **Y** (9 + 5) = _____

H (4 × 4) = _____   **Q** (5 × 1) = _____   **Y** (15 × 1) = _____

H (30 ÷ 2) = _____   **Q** (18 ÷ 3) = _____   **Y** (8 + 8) = _____

H (15 − 10) = _____   **Q** (16 + 6) = _____   **Y** (24 − 7) = _____

An Autumn Holiday

(Thanksgiving)

Use the words from the WORD BANK below. Write all the nouns in the second column. Write adjectives that describe the nouns in the first column.

WORD BANK

friendly	Indians	harvest	sweet	pumpkin	pie
doll	plump	cornhusk	turkey	potatoes	plentiful

Adjectives

1. p _ _ _ _ _ _
2. _ w _ _ _
3. _ _ _ _ _ _ f _ _
4. _ r _ _ _ _ _ _
5. _ _ _ m _
6. _ _ _ _ h _ _ _

Nouns

1. _ _ e
2. _ o _ _ _ _ _ _
3. _ _ _ v _ _ _
4. I _ _ _ _ _ _
5. _ _ r _ _ _
6. _ _ _ I

Now write each noun and adjective pair in a sentence.

1. _____
2. _____
3. _____
4. _____
5. _____
6. _____

November Management

- Clip Art
- Contracts and Awards
- Holiday Report Form
- A Month of Writing
- And More!

Hot Tips!

When you have time to spare before dismissal for lunch or the end of the day, have some fun with this idea. Each student must make up an alliterative sentence that begins with the first letter of their first name. Sara, for example, might say, "It's silly saying such short sentences."

Cut out many samples of clip art. Give one to each student. Have them glue the clip art to a sheet of lined paper, using the art as the focus of a drawing or a story. Time them! Allow ten minutes for a drawing or scene, and fifteen minutes for a written story.

Date _____

A Month of Writing

...n day with a short ...? Every day before the stude... the room, write one of the following topics on the board. The first thing students should do is copy the topic heading on a sheet of paper and list all the sights, sounds, smells, and sensations that have to do with that subject. Compile words into a class Word Bank for creative writing projects.

1.	The Circus	16.	A Snowfall
2.	A Picnic	17.	The School Lunchroom
3.	A Baseball Game	18.	A Fast Food Restaurant
4.	A Movie Theater	19.	A Bakery
5.	The Park	20.	The Seashore
6.	A Birthday Party	21.	A Barn
7.	A Dance	22.	The Airport
8.	A Rainstorm	23.	The Gas Station
9.	A Parade	24.	An Ice Cream Parlor
10.	A Classroom	25.	A Bowling Alley
11.	The Library	26.	The Zoo
12.	The Bus Stop	27.	A Soccer Game
13.	A Convenience Store	28.	A Swimming Pool
14.	The Video Arcade	29.	The Hair Salon/Barber Shop
15.	An Amusement Park	30.	A Shoe Store

Finger Puppets

1. Reproduce on white construction paper.

2. Color and cut out.

3. Cut along dashed lines.

4. Fasten finger puppet around finger with tape.

Indian Place Cards

1. Reproduce on white construction paper, color and cut out.
2. Paste Tab A over Tab B of Base to form a ring. Then cut slits.
3. Place Indian in slits as shown in diagram at the top of the page.

Base

Tab B

Tab A

Pilgrim Place Cards

1. Reproduce on white construction paper, color and cut out.
2. Paste Tab A over Tab B of Base to form a ring. Then cut slits.
3. Place Pilgrim in slits as shown in diagram at the top of the page.

Base

November Record Form

NAME																

Homework!

Write your assignments in the spaces below. Check them off as you complete them.

Reading

Mon. _____

Tues. _____

Wed. _____

Thurs. _____

Fri. _____

Language

Mon. _____

Tues. _____

Wed. _____

Thurs. _____

Fri. _____

Math

Mon. _____

Tues. _____

Wed. _____

Thurs. _____

Fri. _____

Science

Mon. _____

Tues. _____

Wed. _____

Thurs. _____

Fri. _____

Social Studies

Mon. _____

Tues. _____

Wed. _____

Thurs. _____

Fri. _____

Other

Mon. _____

Tues. _____

Wed. _____

Thurs. _____

Fri. _____

#153 November Monthly Activities

Thank You/Invitation

You're Invited

Thank You

Contract/Award

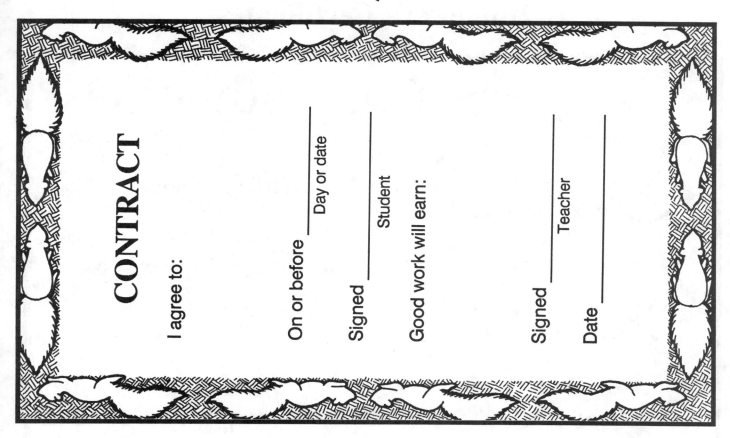

CONTRACT

I agree to:

On or before _____
                   Day or date

Signed _____
                 Student

Good work will earn: _____

Signed _____
                 Teacher

Date _____

AWARD

This is to certify that _____
                                          Name

did **EXCELLENT WORK** in:

Congratulations!

_____
        Teacher

Homework Certificates

Congratulations!

This is to certify that

_____

did the assigned homework on

_____ .

date

_____

Teacher

You Remembered Your Homework!

To: _____

Date: _____

_____

Teacher

We're Going On A Field Trip!

Where: _____

_____

When: _____

_____

Why: _____

_____

How: _____

_____

Please bring: _____

_____

_____

Please sign the permission slip below and have your child return it by _____

_____. Your child will not be allowed to go without the slip.

Thank you.

_____
Teacher

✂--

My child, _____, has my permission to

participate in the field trip to _____.

_____
Parent

☐ I would like to chaperone. Please contact me!

An Alphabetical Book Report

After you have read a book, make an alphabet for it! On each line below write the names of characters, places, events, or vocabulary words from the story that begin with that letter. Share your list with others in the class and see if they can guess the name of the book you read.

A is for _____

B is for _____

C is for _____

D is for _____

E is for _____

F is for _____

G is for _____

H is for _____

I is for _____

J is for _____

K is for _____

L is for _____

M is for _____

N is for _____

O is for _____

P is for _____

Q is for _____

R is for _____

S is for _____

T is for _____

U is for _____

V is for _____

W is for _____

X is for _____

Y is for _____

Z is for _____

58

November Bookmarks

Materials

- *bookmark pattern*
- *tagboard*
- *crayons or colored markers*
- *scissors*

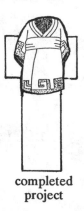

completed
project

Directions

Note: *Make a pattern out of tagboard. Have the child use the pattern to make his own bookmark.*

1. Trace around pattern onto tagboard.

2. Draw an object, animal, or other shape in the square at the top of the bookmark pattern. (Supply the kimono, bookworm, or vote hat patterns below, if desired.)

3. Cut out.

4. Color the design with crayons or marking pens.

bookmark
pattern

 Have students put their sticker awards for the month on the bookmark handle. Stamp awards onto the handle, too.

60

Creative Writing

_____

_____

_____

_____

_____

_____

_____

_____

_____

_____

_____

_____

_____

_____

_____

_____

_____

_____

_____

_____

_____

Name _____   Date _____

Holiday Report

Name of holiday _____

Date it is celebrated _____

Date it was first celebrated _____

Historical events and people that led to its celebration _____

_____

_____

_____

_____

Type of holiday (circle answer):   Local, state, national, religious.

Draw some symbols of this holiday.	List some stories, poems, or songs associated with this holiday.
	_____ _____ _____ _____ _____ _____
This holiday's colors and what they mean. _____ _____ _____ _____ _____ _____	**Traditions, customs, or celebrations associated with this holiday.** _____ _____ _____ _____ _____ _____

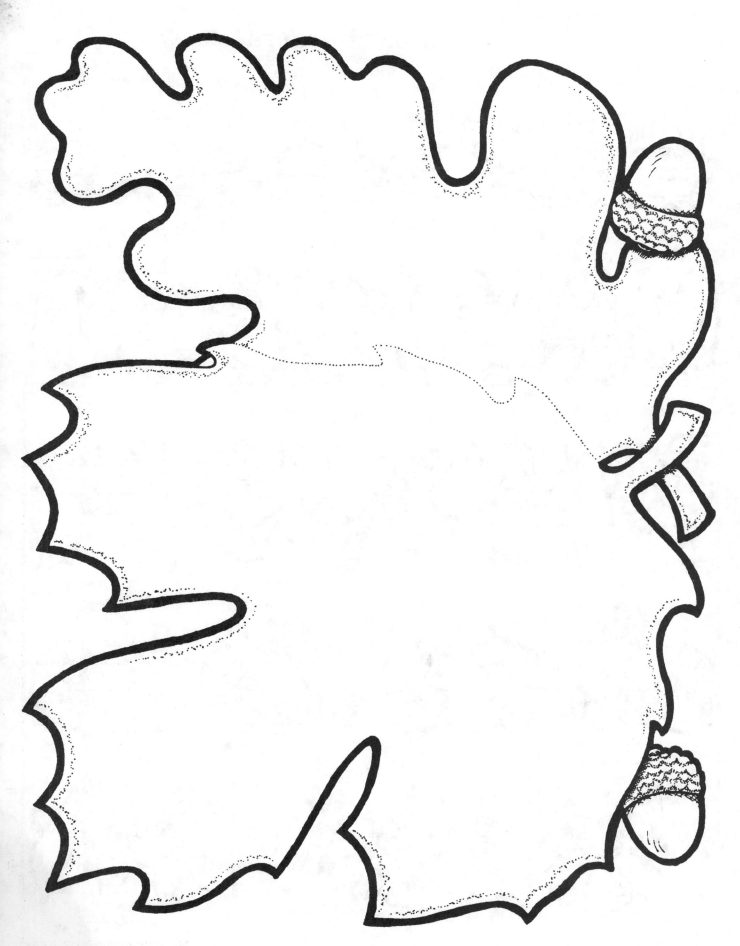

November Borders

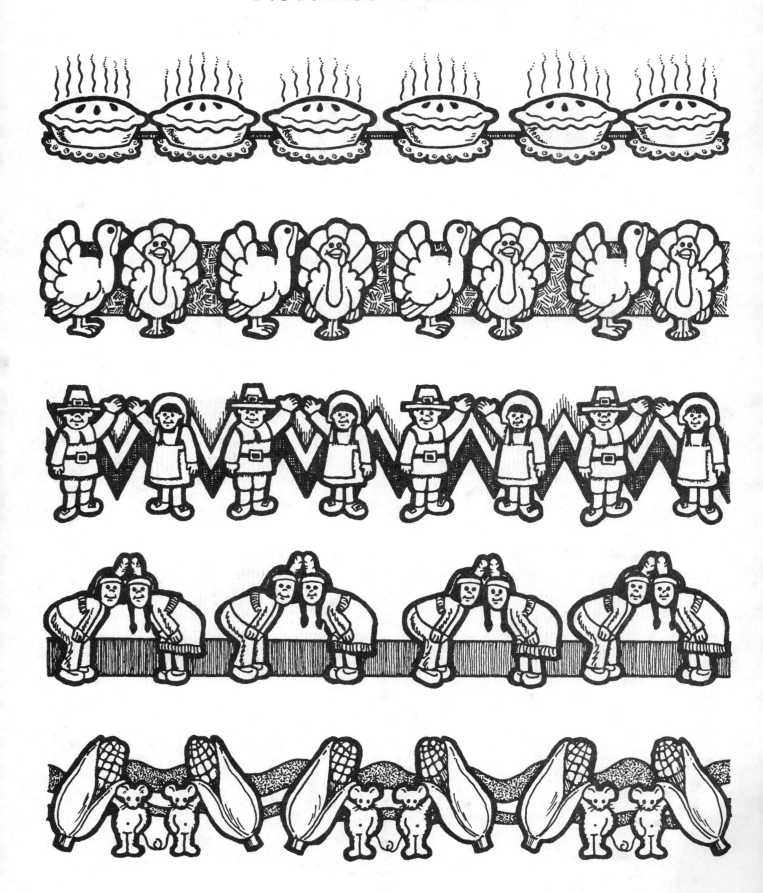

Big Patterns

Big Patterns

Big Patterns

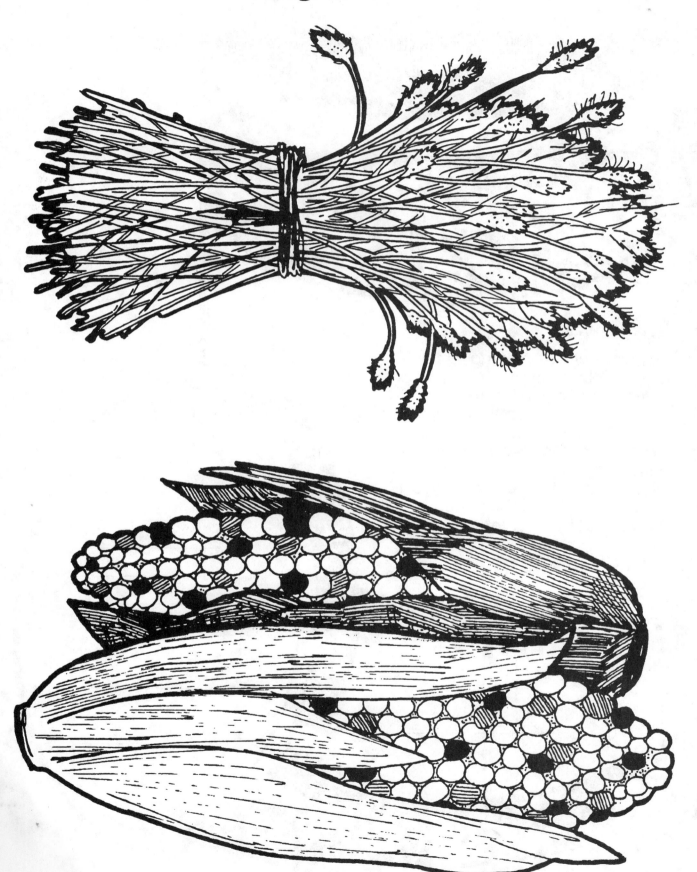

OATMEAL

Dear Parents,

Our class will be making lots of fun projects this month. Many of our activities will require items you may already have at home. Would you please take a minute and see if you have any of the following items on hand? If so, please send them in with your child. Then, keep this list as a reminder to help our class throughout the month.

THANK YOU!

_____
Teacher

68

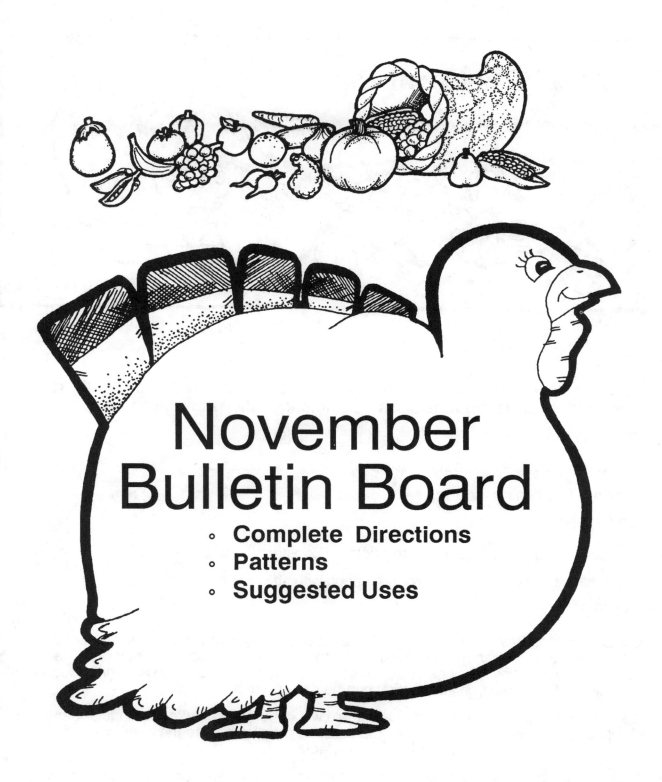

November
Bulletin Board

- ○ **Complete Directions**
- ○ **Patterns**
- ○ **Suggested Uses**

Play a guessing game. Give two or three clues about a fruit or vegetable. Students must guess the answer. For example, "I am green and round like a ball. Who am I?"

Have students group the fruits and vegetables as many different ways as they can. For example, the foods could be grouped according to size, color, how they grow, if they have seeds, ways they can be prepared.

Thanksgiving Cornucopia

OBJECTIVES

This interactive bulletin board can be used to teach or reinforce math, reading, social studies, and language skills. Some suggestions are given below.

MATERIALS

colored construction paper   stapler   scissors

Optional: Push pins; fabric

CONSTRUCTION

- Duplicate patterns onto appropriately colored construction paper; cut out.
- Assemble all pieces onto background; attach with staples or push pins.

DIRECTIONS

- **Food Reports.** Pair students and assign a different fruit or vegetable to each one. Brainstorm questions they have about these foods. For example, how they grow, the varieties of each, ways they can be prepared, etc. Have them choose any three questions to answer. Their research information can be written on their shape.

- **Round It Off!** Label each fruit and vegetable with a numeral. Make rectangular game cards for the answers. Instruct students to round the numbers to the nearest hundred. Match the answer to the correct fruit or vegetable.

- **A Sensory Approach.** Brainstorm with the class. On each fruit or vegetable write words that describe its taste, texture, and appearance. Use the words in research projects and creative writing.

Hot Tips!

 Have the students bring in fresh fruit. Cut them up and make fruit salad. Observe each fruit as it is cut. Do any of them have a similar pattern? Which one is the class favorite? Make a class graph.

Thanksgiving Cornucopia

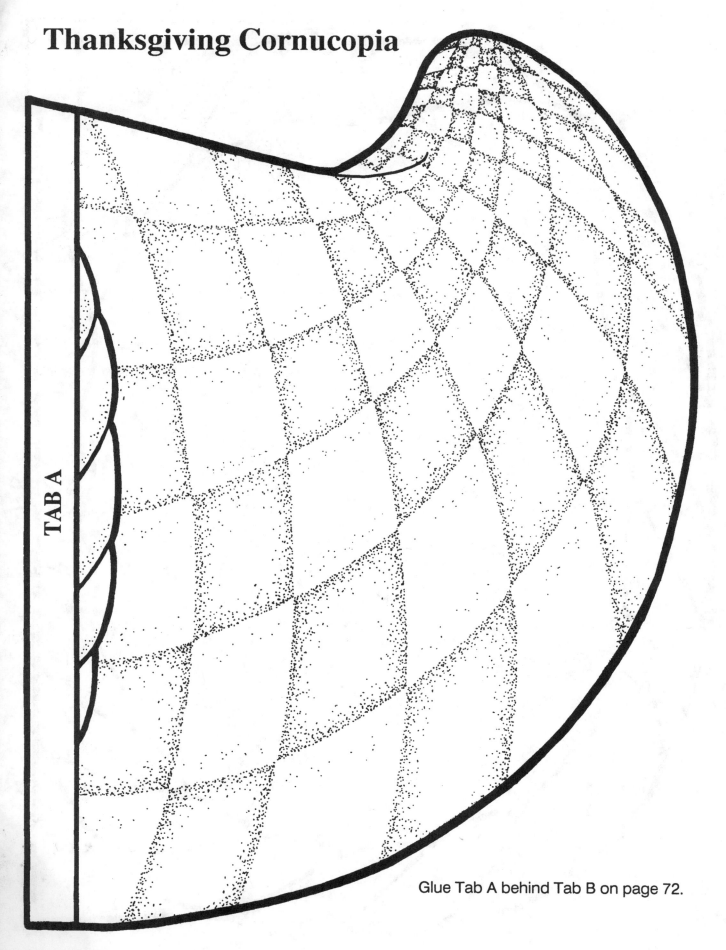

TAB A

Glue Tab A behind Tab B on page 72.

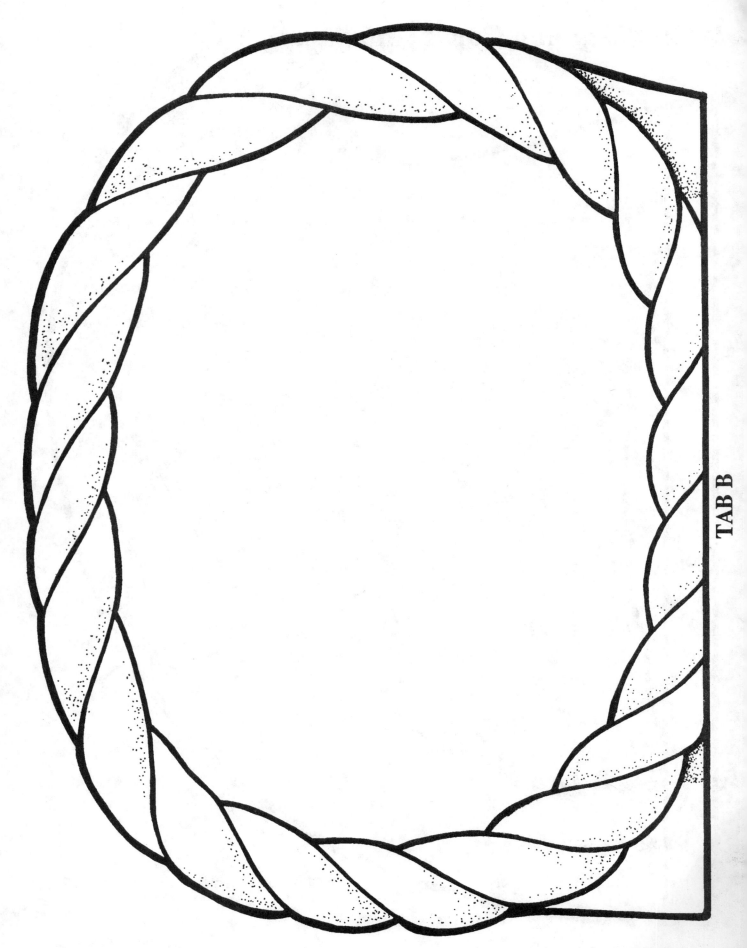

TAB B

Thanksgiving Cornucopia
(cont.)

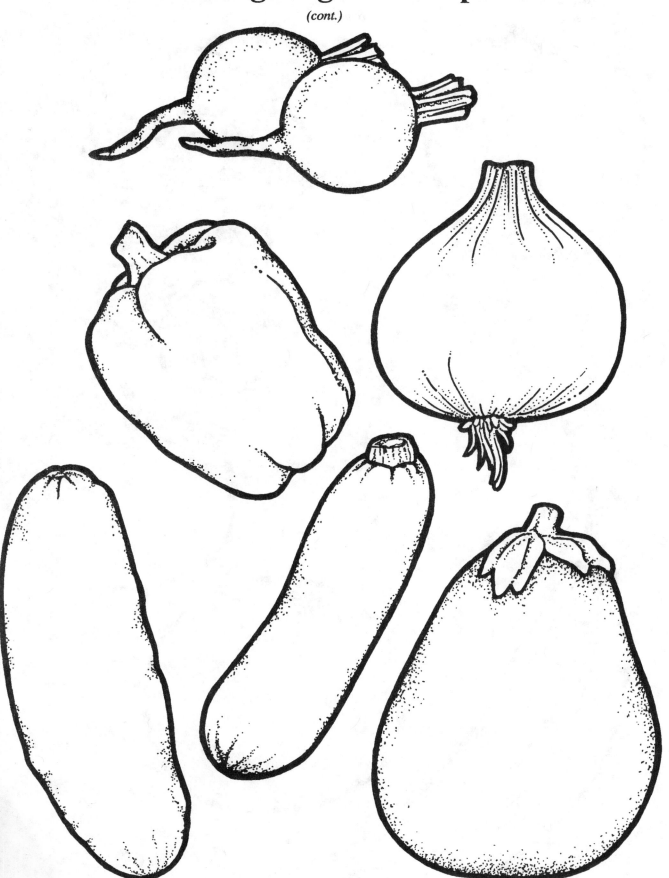

Thanksgiving Cornucopia

(cont.)

Thanksgiving Cornucopia

(cont.)

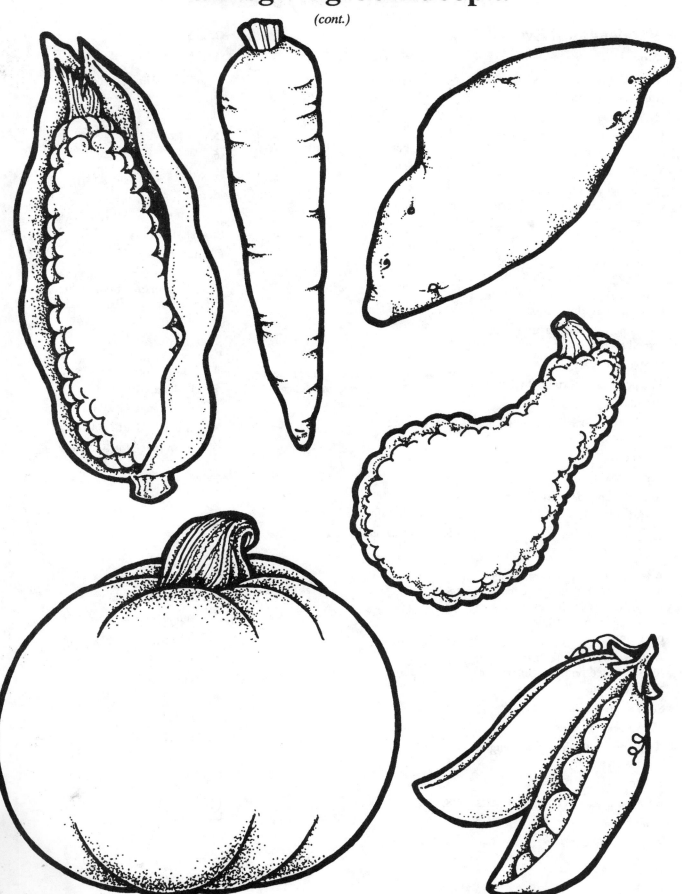

Answer Key

p. 8-9 Calendar of Events

1. Answers will vary
2. South Dakota
3. Answers will vary
4. Egypt
5. Leader of a group that tried to blow up Parliament
6. Piano
7. A scientist who studies the properties and changes of matter and energy
8. Helena
9. Stars, planets and other heavenly bodies and their size, motion, etc.
10. In the early days they wore leather bands around their throats.
11. Someone who has served in the armed forces.
12. Nineteenth
13. The poem's pattern of rhythm
14. Bright
15. A brightly colored robe made of cotton or silk
16. Mistletoe
17. Answers will vary
18. Answer depends on the year
19. Forty
20. Thursday
21. Pine
22. A volunteer program established by President Kennedy; Peace Corps workers help developing countries improve their living conditions.
23. A story, based on historical events, that is passed on from generation to generation.
24. San Diego
25. New York Yankees
26. A person who believes in doing away with slavery
27. History
28. Because of its red colored deserts
29. *Little Women*
30. Samuel Clemens

p. 13

1. 18 triangles
2. 21 squares

p. 15

1. apple
2. pepper
3. tomato
4. carrot
5. grape
6. pear
7. pumpkin
8. cranberry
9. potato
10. pineapple
11. squash
12. corn

p. 25
first, fresh, cob, meat, beans, spoon, plate, lima, corn, cream, butter, pepper

p. 27

1. 10
2. 3
3. Thursday
4. Wednesday
5. Tuesday and Saturday
6. 5
7. 15
8. 20

Challenge: 43

p. 28

1. <
2. <
3. >
4. <
5. >
6. <
7. >
8. <
9. <
10. >
11. >
12. <

p. 34

1. store
2. end
3. binder
4. let
5. worm
6. case
7. mark
8. keeper
9. mobile
10. shelf

Challenge:

bookbinder, bookcase, bookend, booklet, bookmark, bookmobile, bookshelf, bookstore, bookworm

p. 35

1. Pierre, South Dakota
2. Helena, Montana
3. Oklahoma City, Oklahoma
4. Raleigh, North Carolina
5. Bismarck, North Dakota
a. 2
b. 1
c. 5
d. 4
e. 3

p. 36

1. Swiss
2. tomato
3. jelly
4. rye
5. egg
6. cheese
7. steak
8. melt
9. club
10. beef
11. fish
12. salad

Answer Key

(cont.)

p. 37

1. staff
2. clef
3. measure
4. double
5. whole
6. half
7. quarter
8. rest

p. 38 Wordsearch

p. 39

Across:

2. Mercury
3. Uranus
5. Mars
8. Saturn
10. comet
11. Pluto

Down:

1. Venus
4. star
5. moon
6. Jupiter
7. Earth
9. Neptune

p. 41

1. subtraction; 37
2. addition; 13
3. subtraction; depends on this year
4. multiplication; 600
5. division; 10
6. division; 15

p. 43

1. through
2. we
3. horse, way
4. To, sleigh
5. Through
6. wood
8. toes
9. nose

   pay, way, sleigh

   flow, snow, blow, go

   hose, knows, nose, toes

pp. 44, 45 Thanksgiving Graphics

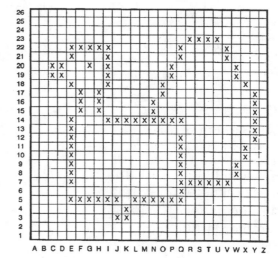

p. 46

1. pumpkin pie
2. sweet potatoes
3. plentiful harvest
4. friendly Indians
5. plump turkey
6. cornhusk doll

   Sentences will vary.

Open Worksheet Skills

These pages are ready to use. Simply fill in the directions and write the skill you want to reinforce. Make a copy for each student or pair of students or glue the worksheet to tagboard and laminate. Place at an appropriate classroom center; students can use water-based pens for easy wipe off and subsequent use. Ideas and resources for programming these worksheets are provided below and on the following pages.

Math

Basic Facts	Sets
Comparing numbers and fractions	missing addends
Decimals	Money problems
Word problems	Geometric shapes
Time	Measurement
Place value	Word names for numbers
Skip counting	Sequence
Ordinal numbers (1st, 2nd, 3rd, etc.)	Percent

Roman Numerals

I - 1	VI - 6	L - 50
II - 2	VII - 7	C - 100
III - 3	VIII - 8	D - 500
IV - 4	IX - 9	M - 1,000
V - 5	X - 10	$\overline{\text{L}}$ - 50,000

Metric Measurement

mm - millimeter (1/10 cm)	g - gram
cm - centimeter (10 mm)	kg - kilogram (1,000 g)
dm - decimeter (10 cm)	1 - liter (1,000 mL)
m - meter (1,000 mm)	mL - mililiter
km - kilometer (1,000 m)	cc - cubic centimeter

Measurement Equivalents

12 in. = 1 ft	4 qt. = 1 gal.	1 t. = 2,000 lbs
3 ft. = 1 yd.	2 pt. = 1 qt.	60 sec. = 1 min.
5,280 ft. = 1 mi.	8 oz. = 1 c.	60 min, = 1 hr.

Open Worksheet Skills

(cont.)

Abbreviations

Names of states	dr. - drive	mt. - mountain
Days of the week	ave. - avenue	p. - page
Units of measurement	Dr. - Doctor	etc. - et cetera
Months of the year	Mrs. - Misses	yr. - year
blvd. - boulevard	Mr. - Mister	wk. - week
rd. - road	Gov. - Governor	
st. - street	Pres. - President	

Contractions

isn't - is not	I've - I have	they'd - they would
doesn't - does not	we've - we have	you'll - you will
haven't - have not	I'm - I am	won't - will not
hasn't - has not	you're - you are	I'm - I am
that's - that is	it's - it is	let's - let us

Compound Words

airplane	bodyguard	everywhere	percent
anyhow	bookcase	footnote	quarterback
anything	cardboard	grandfather	snowflake
basketball	classroom	handwriting	suitcase
bedroom	earthquake	makeup	watermelon

Prefixes

dis -	un -	over -	re -
disapprove	uncut	overcharge	recover
discolor	uneven	overdressed	redo
discount	unfair	overdue	reheat
dislike	unhappy	overfeed	remiss
dismay	unlike	overgrown	replay
dismiss	unmade	overpaid	reset
disobey	unwashed	overrun	review

Suffixes

- ful	- less	- ly	- en
beautiful	ageless	actively	harden
careful	homeless	happily	moisten
helpful	priceless	quickly	sweeten
skillful	worthless	silently	thicken

Open Worksheet Skills

(cont.)

Plurals

- s		- es		- ies	
toe	kitten	church	class	sky	cherry
pin	window	lunch	inch	baby	body
lamp	star	box	tomato	party	army
book	key	brush	waltz	family	lady

Anagrams

dear - dare - read	shoe - hoes - hose	veto - vote
notes - stone - tones	vase - save	cone - once
fowl - flow - wolf	pea - ape	stop - tops - pots - post - spot
veil - vile - evil - live	north - thorn	steam - meats - mates -
tea - ate - eat	flea - leaf	tames

Synonyms

sleepy - tired	wealthy - rich	friend - pal
firm - solid	quick - fast	tiny - small
story - tale	sea - ocean	jump - leap
shut - close	icy - cold	gift - present
easy - simple	chore - task	hike - walk

Antonyms

empty - full	tall - short	correct - wrong
tame - wild	rough - smooth	forget - remember
city - country	light - dark	thick - slender
faster - slower	dirty - clean	sweet - sour
strong - weak	calm - nervous	young - aged

Homonyms

eight - ate	pale - pail	by - buy - bye
whole - hole	knew - new	sense - cents - scents
red - read	nose - knows	two - too - to
hour - our	blew - blue	
peace - piece	would - wood	
lone - loan	for - four - fore	